National Gang Threat Assessment

The National Gang Intelligence Center thanks the National Drug Intelligence Center for collecting and analyzing strategic gang-related intelligence and producing this document.

NATIONAL GANG THREAT ASSESSMENT

National Gang Threat Summary

Gangs pose a serious threat to public safety in many communities throughout the United States. Gang members are increasingly migrating from urban to suburban areas and are responsible for a growing percentage of crime and violence in many communities. Much gang-related criminal activity involves drug trafficking; however, gang members are increasingly engaging in alien and weapons trafficking. Additionally, a rising number of U.S.-based gangs are seemingly intent on developing working relationships with U.S.- and foreign-based drug trafficking organizations (DTOs) and other criminal organizations to gain direct access to foreign sources of illicit drugs.

Key Findings

The following key findings were developed by analysis of available federal, state, and local law enforcement information; 2008 National Drug Intelligence Center (NDIC) National Drug Threat Survey (NDTS) data; and verified open source information:

- Approximately 1 million gang members belonging to more than 20,000 gangs were criminally active within all 50 states and the District of Columbia as of September 2008.
- Local street gangs, or neighborhood-based street gangs, remain a significant threat because they continue to account for the largest number of gangs nationwide. Most engage in violence in conjunction with a variety of crimes, including retail-level drug distribution.
- According to NDTS data, 58 percent of state and local law enforcement agencies reported that criminal gangs were active in their jurisdictions in 2008 compared with 45 percent of state and local agencies in 2004.
- Gang members are migrating from urban areas to suburban and rural communities, expanding the gangs' influence in most regions; they are doing so for a variety of reasons, including expanding drug distribution territories, increasing illicit revenue, recruiting new members, hiding from law enforcement, and escaping other gangs. Many suburban and rural communities are experiencing increasing gang-related crime and violence because of expanding gang influence.
- Criminal gangs commit as much as 80 percent of the crime in many communities, according to law enforcement officials throughout the nation. Typical gang-related crimes include alien smuggling, armed robbery, assault, auto theft, drug trafficking, extortion, fraud, home invasions, identity theft, murder, and weapons trafficking.
- Gang members are the primary retail-level distributors of most illicit drugs. They also are increasingly distributing wholesale-level quantities of marijuana and cocaine in most urban and suburban communities.
- Some gangs traffic illicit drugs at the regional and national levels; several are capable of competing with U.S.-based Mexican DTOs.

- U.S.-based gang members illegally cross the U.S.–Mexico border for the express purpose of smuggling illicit drugs and illegal aliens from Mexico into the United States.
- Many gangs actively use the Internet to recruit new members and to communicate with members in other areas of the United States and in foreign countries.
- Street gangs and outlaw motorcycle gangs pose a growing threat to law enforcement along the U.S.– Canada border. They frequently associate with Canada-based gangs and criminal organizations to facilitate various criminal activities, including drug smuggling into the United States.

Table of Contents

PREFACE

This intelligence assessment is a collaborative effort between the National Gang Intelligence Center (NGIC) and the NDIC to examine the threat posed to the United States by criminal gangs; it supports U.S. Department of Justice strategic objectives 2.2 (to reduce the threat, incidence, and prevalence of violent crime) and 2.4 (to reduce the threat, trafficking, use, and related violence of illegal drugs). The assessment is based on federal, state, and local law enforcement information and is supplemented by information retrieved from open sources. Information and data used for this report were collected through September 2008.

This assessment discusses the proliferation of gangs from urban areas to suburban and rural locations, estimates of the number of gangs and gang members in the United States, gang types, gang-related criminal activities, locations where specific gangs operate, and the relationships between gangs and other criminal organizations. Regional summaries highlighting the most significant gang-related trends are also provided. The assessment also identifies intelligence gaps and provides predictive estimates regarding significant gang-related issues.

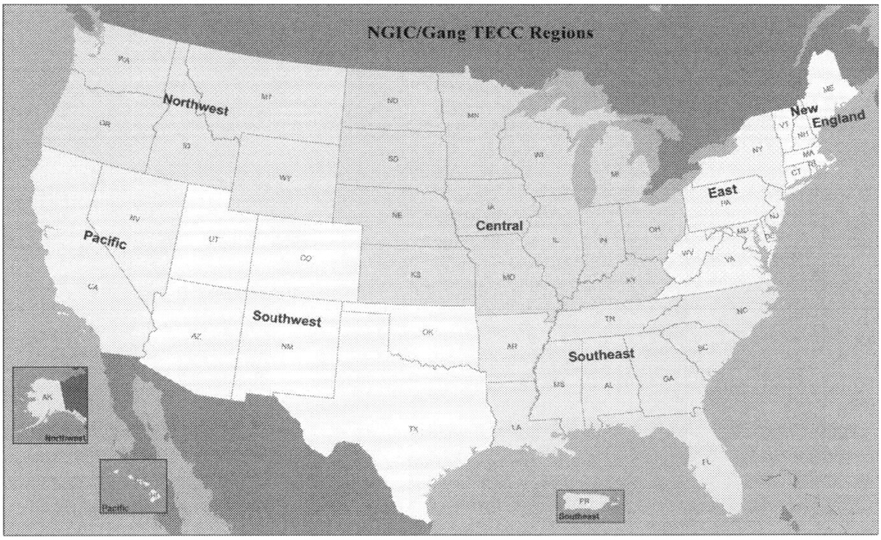

Figure 1. National Gang Intelligence Center/National Gang Targeting, Enforcement & Coordination Center Regions.

National Gang Intelligence Center

The NGIC is a multiagency effort that integrates the gang intelligence assets of federal, state, and local law enforcement entities to serve as a centralized intelligence resource for gang information and analytical support. The mission of the NGIC is to support law enforcement agencies through timely and accurate information sharing and strategic/tactical analysis of federal, state, and local law enforcement intelligence focusing on the growth, migration, criminal activity, and association of gangs that pose a significant threat to communities throughout the United States. The NGIC concentrates on gangs operating on a national level that demonstrate criminal connectivity between sets and common identifiers and goals. Because many violent gangs do not operate on a national level, the NGIC also focuses on regional-level gangs. NGIC is staffed and supported by a number of partnering agencies, including the Bureau of Alcohol, Tobacco, Firearms, and Explosives (ATF), Bureau of Prisons (BOP), Department of Justice (DOJ), Department of Homeland Security (DHS), Customs and Border Protection (CBP), Drug Enforcement Administration (DEA), Federal Bureau of Investigation (FBI), Immigration and Customs Enforcement (ICE), NDIC, and United States Marshals Service (USMS). The NGIC produces intelligence assessments, intelligence bulletins, joint agency intelligence products, and other nonstandard intelligence products for customers.

GangTECC

The National Gang Targeting, Enforcement & Coordination Center (GangTECC) began operations in summer 2006 as the national anti-gang task force created by the former Attorney General. In accordance with the former Attorney General's directive, GangTECC is a multiagency center designed to serve as a critical catalyst in a unified federal effort to help disrupt and dismantle the most significant and violent gangs in the United States. The senior investigators at GangTECC come from the ATF, BOP, DEA, FBI, USMS, and ICE at the Department of Homeland Security. These federal agents work in close collaboration with the Gang Squad prosecutors in the Criminal Division of the Department of Justice and with the analysts and others at the NGIC. They are among the primary consumers of NGIC intelligence. Specifically, GangTECC:

- Assists the initiation of gang-related investigations and enhances existing investigations and prosecutions.
- Aids in the coordination, deconfliction, and effectiveness of gang-related initiatives, investigations, and prosecutions.
- Develops an enhanced understanding of the national gang problem and proposes strategies to neutralize the most violent and significant threats.
- Coordinates with and supports the NGIC.

The goal is to achieve maximum impact at the national level against the most violent gangs in this country. To further this goal, GangTECC is intended to provide "one-stop shopping" via phone and e-mail for local, state, and federal investigators and prosecutors engaged in significant anti-gang efforts. GangTECC, through the participation of its member agencies, can offer either direct support for those engaged in anti-gang initiatives or can connect interested parties to appropriate officials to provide guidance or assistance. In many instances, specific assistance, coordination, or access to information developed in related cases would be invaluable to an ongoing gang investigation or prosecution.

Scope and Methodology

The principal sources of information used in this assessment include:

- 3,052 state and local law enforcement agency responses to the 2008 NDIC NDTS.
- Information from other federal, state, and local law enforcement agencies.
- Gang-related federal criminal investigative information.

One of the greatest impediments to the collection of accurate gang-related data is the lack of a national uniform definition of a gang used by all federal, state, and local law enforcement agencies. For the purpose of this assessment, the National Alliance of Gang Investigators' Associations (NAGIA) definition[1] is used: A gang is a group or association of three or more persons with a common identifying sign, symbol, or name who individually or collectively engage in criminal activity that creates an atmosphere of fear and intimidation. Another obstacle to the collection of gang-related data is the denial of a gang presence by local officials in some jurisdictions despite indicators to the contrary.

Gangs also are defined by the geographic areas in which they operate. Local gangs, also called neighborhood-based gangs and neighborhood drug crews, operate in single locations. Local gangs usually have no direct ties to DTOs or other criminal organizations. Regional gangs operate in multiple locations within a region; these gangs communicate and associate with gang members in other locations to varying degrees. Regional gangs typically are organized more formally and have more members than local gangs; some have members in foreign countries. Members of regional gangs may maintain ties to DTOs and other criminal organizations operating in the United States. National gangs typically have several hundred to several thousand members nationwide who operate in multiple regions; they may have cells in foreign countries with members who assist the U.S.-based gangs in further developing associations with DTOs and other criminal organizations in those countries. The organizational structures of national gangs vary from loosely linked networks of cells to formal hierarchies.

The collection of gang-related data for this assessment was greatly strengthened by the relatively large number of NDTS responses (3,052). Preparation of this assessment also was aided by better reporting as a result of, in part, the success of DOJ Office Justice Programs (OJP)/Bureau of Justice Assistance (BJA) grants and training; FBI, ATF, and DEA enforcement; NDIC, NGIC, and El Paso Intelligence Center (EPIC) intelligence and reporting; and GangTECC targeting and coordination.

1 For this report, the National Alliance of Gang Investiga-tors' Association (NAGIA) definition of "gang" is used as it is commonly accepted by gang investigator associations throughout the country. However, many states have leg-islatively enacted definitions of gangs that most local and state law enforcement agencies are required to follow.

KEY QUESTIONS

Analysts used these key questions to frame the discussions in this assessment:

- What threat do gangs pose at the national and regional levels?
- How many gangs and gang members are in existence, and where are they located?
- Which gangs pose the greatest threat?
- Which gangs have ties to drug trafficking and transnational organizations?
- What types of criminal activity do gang members engage in?

KEY ASSUMPTIONS

Analysts made the following assumptions in the production of this assessment:

- The term "gang," for analytical purposes, has the same meaning across local, state, and federal jurisdictions, although legislation in various jurisdictions may define the term in a slightly different manner.
- The number of gang members in a particular jurisdiction was estimated at the mean of the range reported by that jurisdiction in response to the 2008 NDIC NDTS.

GANG PROLIFERATION

Gang migration from urban communities to suburban and rural locations, which began more than two decades ago, is a significant and growing problem in most areas of the country. Gangs are now fully entrenched in many communities across the nation. Most gangs formed in major cities and expanded into neighboring communities during the 1970s, continued their expansion in the 1980s, and launched into full-scale migration during the 1990s. Many notable gangs, such as Chicago-based Gangster Disciples, Black P. Stones, and Latin Kings, initially formed as organizations for political and social reform during the 1960s. However, by the early 1970s the focus of a number of these gangs shifted from reform to criminal activity for profit. At this time gang activity was primarily confined to large cities.

Throughout the 1970s gangs became better organized and continued to expand their activities into neighboring communities. The movement of gang members to suburban areas resulted in some territorial conflicts between rival gang members competing for the new territory, in addition to territorial conflicts with the few existing suburban gang members. The gang members who migrated from urban areas often formed new, neighborhood-based local gangs. These local gangs generally controlled their territories through violence and intimidation. In addition, they sought to increase their size by recruiting new members, who were typically from single-parent, low-income households, and who had a limited education. Local gangs engaged in a wide range of criminal activity, including retail-level drug distribution.

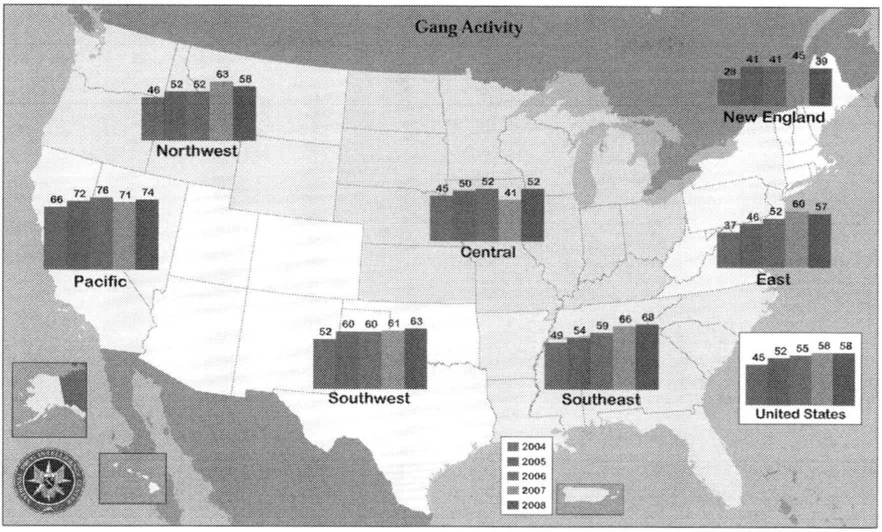

Figure 2. Percentage of State and Local Law Enforcement Agencies Reporting Gang Activity, by Region.

Source: National Drug Threat Survey 2004–2008.

During the 1980s, gangs that engaged in drug trafficking in major cities began to expand their drug distribution networks into suburban communities influenced by local gangs. The larger gangs controlled drug distribution in city drug markets; they were motivated to move into adjoining communities to generate additional income by capitalizing on burgeoning powder cocaine and crack cocaine abuse. Large urban gangs generated millions of dollars from trafficking illicit drugs in urban and suburban areas; this income enabled the gangs to recruit new members and to force smaller local gangs to either disband or align with them, thereby increasing their dominance. To enhance profits from drug trafficking and other crimes, large urban gangs also deployed members to locate new drug markets throughout the country, including in suburban and rural communities. As various gangs attempted to expand nationally, they often were met with initial resistance by local gangs. This resistance resulted in an increased number of homicides and drive-by shootings in suburban communities.

Gangs became entrenched in communities throughout the nation, and gang-related violence and drug trafficking became fully ingrained in suburban areas throughout the 1990s. Because of the significant levels of violence attendant to gang-related criminal activity, federal, state, and local law enforcement officials devoted significant resources to fighting gun crime and disrupting the most violent gangs. This crackdown on violent gang activity targeted key gang leaders in an effort to dismantle highly structured gangs. In conjunction with this crackdown, federal law enforcement officials began to target violent gang members from Mexico and Central America, most of whom were in the United States illegally. Moreover, a large number of gang members in prison formed associations along ethnic lines during this time in an attempt to protect their operations, giving rise to large, influential prison gangs. As these gang members were released from prison, they maintained contact with gang leaders in prison and used their influence to control street gangs in urban and suburban areas.

Gang migration from larger cities to suburban and rural areas is an ongoing concern for law enforcement. According to analysis of NDTS 2008 data, the percentage of law enforcement agencies in the United States reporting gang activity in their jurisdictions increased from 45 percent in 2004 to 58 percent in 2008. (See Figure 2 on page 4.) Moreover, the percentage of jurisdictions reporting gang activity during this time frame increased in each of the seven NGIC/Gang TECC regions; however, the most significant increases were in the East and Southeast Regions, most likely the result of the migration of gang members from urban areas such as New York, New York; Chicago, Illinois; and Los Angeles, California, to smaller jurisdictions in these regions. In Chicago, gang movement to suburban areas can be attributed to several factors: the breakdown of traditional hierarchical gang structures resulting from law enforcement targeting of gang leaders, the razing of some large Chicago public housing projects, an abundance of wholesale illicit drug suppliers, and the expectation of high profits from new suburban drug operations.

Figure 3. Percentage of Students Reporting Gang Activity at Schools

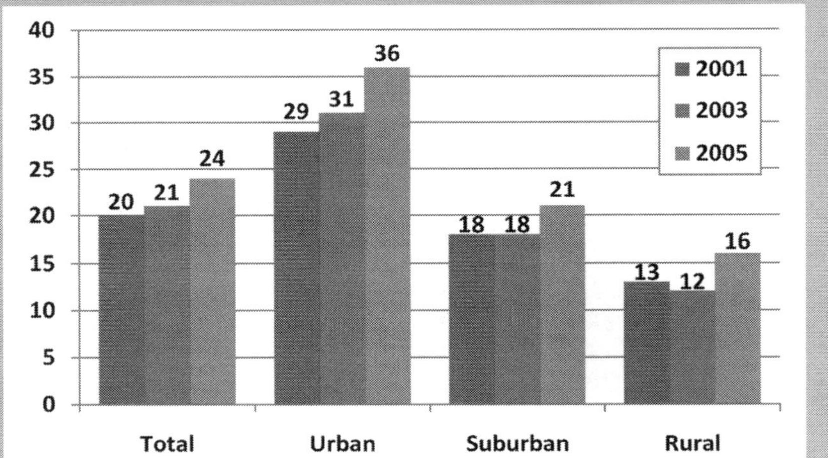

Source: National Crime Victimization Survey.
Note: *Indicators of School Crime and Safety: 2007* is a joint annual report by the Bureau of Justice Statistics and the National Center for Education Statistics. The *School Crime Supplement* to the *National Crime Victimization Survey* is biennial.

Gang migration from urban areas has led to the recruitment of new, younger gang members in many suburban and rural communities. According to the most recent biennial School Crime Supplement to the Bureau of Justice Statistics (BJS) National Crime Victimization Survey,[2] the percentage of suburban students ages 12-18 who reported that gangs were present at school during the previous 6 months increased 17 percent from 2003 to 2005 after remaining stable from 2001 to 2003, and the percentage of rural students reporting likewise increased 33 percent from 2003 to 2005 after decreasing (8%) from 2001 to 2003. In comparison, percentages of both total students and urban students reporting gangs present at school increased steadily from 2001 to 2005 (20% and 24%, respectively). (See Figure 3 on page 5.) Gang activity at schools is rising, in part, because gangs are using middle schools and high schools as venues for recruitment and drug distribution. Law enforcement agencies in several jurisdictions in eastern states report that gangs are directing teenage members who had dropped out of school to reenroll, primarily to recruit new members and sell drugs.

Gang Membership

Gang membership in the United States was conservatively estimated at 1 million members as of September 2008, based on analysis of federal, state, and local law enforcement reporting—an increase from an estimated 800,000 members in 2005. Current estimates include approximately 900,000 gang members residing within local communities across the country and more than 147,000 documented gang members incarcerated in federal, state, and local correctional facilities, according to state and federal corrections data. Increased gang membership is most likely the result of gang recruitment efforts and the release of incarcerated gang members; however, more comprehensive law enforcement reporting and improved gang awareness may also have contributed to an increase in the number of gang members identified by some law enforcement agencies.

Regionally, gang membership varies significantly. States in the Pacific, Southwest, and Central Regions rank highest in the percentage of the population identified as gang members. (See Appendix A, Map 1.) In addition, these same regions have the highest ratio of gang members per law enforcement officer. (See Appendix A, Map 2.)

Gang Types

Gangs vary extensively regarding membership, structure, age, and ethnicity. However, three basic types of gangs have been identified by gang investigators: street gangs, prison gangs, and outlaw motorcycle gangs (OMGs).

---

2. In 2005, the unit response rate for this survey did not meet the National Center for Education Statistics statistical standards; therefore, interpret the data with caution. Data for 2005 is for the 2005-2006 school year. The biennial data for 2007 is for the 2007-2008 school year and has not been released. For more information on 2005, see Indica-tors of School Crime and Safety: 2007, Appendix A, avail-able at http://www.ojp.usdoj.gov/bjs/pub/pdf/iscs07.pdf.

Street Gangs

Street gangs that operate throughout most of the country are a significant threat because they are the largest and control the greatest geographical area. Therefore, criminal activities such as violence and drug trafficking perpetrated by street gangs pose the greatest threat. The threat becomes magnified as national-and regional-level street gangs migrate from urban areas to suburban and rural communities, expanding their influence in most regions and broadening their presence outside the United States to develop associations with DTOs and other criminal organizations in Mexico, Central America, and Canada.

- Currently, 11 *national-level street gangs* have been identified in the United States, and associates or members have been identified in foreign countries, according to analysis of federal, state, and local law enforcement information. (See Appendix B.) Established cells in foreign countries assist gangs operating in the United States in further developing associations with DTOs and other criminal organizations in those countries. National gangs typically have several hundred to several thousand members nationwide who operate in multiple regions; they may have cells in foreign countries with members who assist the U.S.-based gangs, further developing associations with DTOs and other criminal organizations in those countries.
- *Regional-level street gangs*[3] increasingly distribute drugs at the wholesale level. At least five street gangs, specifically Florencia 13, Fresno Bulldogs, Latin Disciples, Tango Blast, and United Blood Nation, have been identified as operating at a regional-level. (See Appendix B.) Typically, regional-level gangs are organized, with several hundred to several thousand members. Regional-level gangs may have some members in foreign countries and maintain ties to DTOs and other criminal organizations operating in the United States.
- *Local street gangs*, occasionally referred to as neighborhood-based gangs or neighborhood-based drug crews, pose a considerable problem for local law enforcement and a concern for federal law enforcement. Currently, most street gangs are local-level gangs that operate in single locations. Local street gangs usually range in membership from three to several hundred members. Most of these gangs engage in violence in conjunction with a variety of crimes, including retail-level drug distribution; however, they usually have no direct ties to DTOs or other criminal organizations. However, several law enforcement agencies have reported that a few local gangs have established ties to wholesale-level drug traffickers operating along the U.S.–Mexico border. In addition, law enforcement officials in communities along the U.S.–Mexico border have noted an increase in the number of local gang members establishing dual membership with their counterpart gangs in Mexico.

3. Local and regional street gangs, except for a few signifi-cant regional-level gangs, are too numerous to list in Appen-dix B and are, therefore, referenced wherever applicable.

Prison Gangs

Prison gangs pose a serious domestic threat, particularly national-level prison gangs that affiliate with Mexican DTOs and maintain substantial influence over street gangs in the communities in which they operate. Prison gangs are highly structured criminal networks that operate within the federal and state prison systems. Furthermore, these gangs operate in local communities through members who have been released from prison. Released members typically return to their home communities and resume their former street gang affiliations, acting as representatives of their prison gang to recruit street gang members who perform criminal acts on behalf of the prison gang.

Prison gangs often control drug distribution within correctional facilities and heavily influence street-level distribution in some communities. Prison gangs exert considerable control over midlevel and retail-level drug distribution in the Southwest Region and in southern California. Their trafficking activities are facilitated through their connections to Mexican DTOs, which ensure access to a continuous supply of illicit drugs that are distributed through their networks in prison or are supplied to affiliated street gangs.

- *National-level prison gangs* pose a significant threat, since most maintain some type of relationship with DTOs. (See Appendix C.) Of the five identified national-level prison gangs, two have members or associates in at least two foreign countries. Prison gangs are well organized and governed by established sets of rules and codes of conduct that are rigorously enforced by gang leaders. For example, California-based Mexican Mafia (La Eme) uses fear and intimidation to control Hispanic street gangs whose members are in prison and on the street in California. Such control gives La Eme command over 50,000 to 75,000 Sureños gang members and associates.
- *Regional-level prison gangs* pose a more modest, but growing, threat because they are increasingly developing associations with DTOs. Regional-level prison gangs have organizational structures that are similar to those of national-level gangs but typically are limited to operating in one or two state prison systems. The most significant regional-level prison gangs operate in Texas, and most have ties to at least one Mexican DTO.
- *Local- or state-level prison gangs*, particularly those operating along the U.S.–Mexico border, pose a serious concern to local law enforcement officials. Some local prison gangs along the U.S.–Mexico border maintain long-standing ties to Mexican DTOs. Local prison gangs typically operate within the department of corrections in a single state. As members are released from prison, they often settle in local communities in which they recruit and associate with local street gang members and conduct criminal activities on behalf of the prison gang.

OUTLAW MOTORCYCLE GANGS

OMG-related criminal activity poses a threat to public safety in local communities in which these gangs operate because of their wide-ranging criminal activity, propensity to use violence, and ability to counter law enforcement efforts. OMGs are highly structured criminal organizations whose members engage in criminal activities such as violent crime, weapons trafficking, and drug trafficking. OMGs maintain a strong centralized leadership that implements rules regulating membership, conduct, and criminal activity. As of June 2008 state and local law enforcement agencies estimate that between 280 and 520 OMGs are operating at the national, regional, and local levels. OMGs range in size from a single chapter to hundreds of chapters worldwide. Current law enforcement intelligence estimates indicate that more than 20,000 validated OMG members, divided among hundreds of OMGs, reside in the United States.

- *National-level OMG* criminal activity poses a serious national domestic threat. National-level OMGs are a considerable concern to law enforcement because they are highly structured organizations with memberships ranging into the thousands, maintaining strong associations with transnational DTOs and other criminal organizations. In addition, national-level OMGs maintain criminal networks of regional and local motorcycle clubs, commonly referred to as "support," "puppet," or "duck" clubs, whose members conduct criminal activities in support of the larger OMGs, and who are a source for new members.[4] Some members of support clubs have acquired employment with private businesses or government agencies, which enables them to provide national-level OMGs with business, government, and financial information that can be used to protect their criminal enterprises, according to open source and published law enforcement information.
- *Regional-level OMGs* are highly structured organizations that range in size from 50 to several hundred members. In the United States 109 regional-level OMGs have been identified by gang investigators; most support one of the national-level OMGs. Several regional-level OMGs maintain independent associations with transnational DTOs and other criminal organizations.
- *Local-level OMGs* typically operate in a single state or in a few neighboring states and have fewer than 50 members. They are often support clubs for regional- and national-level OMGs. Local-level OMGs usually have no ties to DTOs or to other criminal organizations

4. The term "support club" refers to smaller gangs whose members regularly associate with or are friends of one of the national-level gangs.

CRIMINAL ACTIVITIES

Gangs are responsible for a significant portion of the crime in many urban communities and in an increasing number of suburban communities across the country; much of this crime is associated with their drug trafficking activities. According to local law enforcement information, gang members are responsible for as much as 80 percent of the crime in some locations.[5] [5]Violent disputes over control of drug territory and enforcement of drug debts frequently occur among street gangs in urban areas and, increasingly, in suburban communities where gangs have expanded their drug distribution operations. Gang members also engage in a host of other criminal activities such as auto theft, assault, alien smuggling, burglary, drive-by shootings, extortion, firearms offenses, home invasion robberies, homicide, identity theft, insurance fraud, mortgage fraud, operating prostitution rings, and weapons trafficking.

Drug distribution by gang members poses a growing concern in suburban and rural communities; gang members are the primary retail-level drug distributors and are increasing their wholesale-level drug distribution in most urban and suburban communities. According to the NDTS 2008, 58 percent of law enforcement agencies in the United States report that gangs are involved in drug distribution, compared with 45 percent in 2004; much of this increase occurred in suburban and rural areas. NDTS data further indicate that the primary drug distributed by gangs is marijuana, followed by powder cocaine, crack cocaine, MDMA (3,4-methylenedioxymethamphetamine, also known as ecstasy), methamphetamine, diverted pharmaceuticals, and heroin. (See Figure 4.)Open source reporting indicates that gang-related violent crime is increasing in some urban areas. For example, in San Diego, California, fatal gang-related homicides increased 56 percent from 18 in 2006 to 28 in 2007. In addition, Salinas, California, gang-related homicides increased 125 percent from 4 in 2006 to 9 in 2007.

Law enforcement agencies report that gang members are increasingly using firearms in conjunction with their criminal activities. Moreover, during the latest 5-year reporting period ending in 2007, 94.3 percent of gang-related homicides reportedly involved the use of a firearm. Gang members typically buy, sell, and trade firearms among their associates. Gang members often obtain these firearms through thefts and straw purchases. These firearms are for personal use or for use by fellow gang members in committing homicides and armed robberies. For example, members and associates of Los Angeles-based Black P Stone Bloods and Rolling 20s Crips were arrested in July 2008 for illegally selling more than 119 firearms, according to law enforcement reporting. In addition, members of California-based Mara Salvatrucha obtain weapons for their personal use and sell weapons and ammunition to members of other gangs in California for profit, according to FBI information.

5. Stated percentage is based solely on self-reporting by local law enforcement. The figures given are not meant to represent an National Drug Intelligence Center (NDIC) analysis.

Figure 4. Percentage of Law Enforcement Agencies Reporting Gang Involvement in Drug Distribution, by Drug Type, 2004–2008

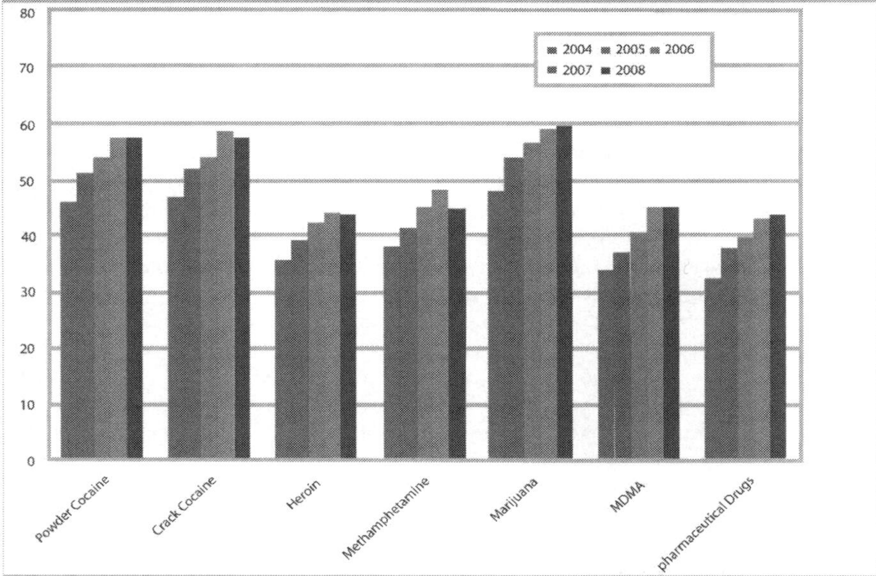

Source: National Drug Threat Survey 2004–2008.

Illicit Finance

Gangs earn the profits essential to maintaining their criminal operations and the lifestyles of their members primarily through drug distribution. Most gang members are retail-level dealers who use drug proceeds to make typical consumer purchases, pay their living costs, or purchase luxury goods such as vehicles and jewelry.

According to openly published law enforcement reporting, gang members typically launder profits from criminal activities through front companies and real estate investments. Gang members use front companies such as clothing stores, hair salons, and music recording and production companies to commingle illicit proceeds earned from drug sales with licit income from these businesses. Some gang members also use mortgage fraud schemes or purchase real estate as investments or as a means to commingle illicit funds with rental payments. For example, members of Chicago-based Latin Kings, Black Disciples, Vice Lords, and Gangster Disciples use mortgage fraud schemes that employ straw purchasers and unscrupulous mortgage brokers and appraisers to purchase properties at a minimal cost and sell them at a higher value to a third party. The gang members receive the profits from the sales, seemingly legitimizing the income, while their associates typically default on the loans, often defrauding banks or mortgage companies.

Gang Communications

Gang members often use cell phones and the Internet to communicate and promote their illicit activities. Street gangs typically use the voice and text messaging capabilities of cell phones to conduct drug transactions and prearrange meetings with customers. Members of street gangs use multiple cell phones that they frequently discard while conducting their drug trafficking operations. For example, the leader of an African American street gang operating on the north side of Milwaukee used more than 20 cell phones to coordinate drug-related activities of the gang; most were prepaid phones that the leader routinely discarded and replaced. Internet-based methods such as social networking sites, encrypted e-mail, Internet telephony, with drug customers. Gang members use social networking Internet sites such as MySpace, YouTube, and Facebook as well as personal web pages to communicate and boast about their gang membership and related activities.

- According to open source and local law enforcement reporting, members of Crips gangs in Hampton, Virginia, use the Internet to intimidate rival gang members and maintain web sites to recruit new members. On October 23, 2007, a 15-year-old Crips gang member was arrested for shooting a rival gang member in the leg. Additionally, he was charged with the recruitment of persons for a criminal street gang through the use of the gang's social networking site.
- Gangs in Oceanside, California, are recruiting new members and claiming new turf on the Internet. Gang members flash gang signs and wear gang colors in videos and photos displayed on Internet sites. Sometimes, rivals "spar" on Internet message boards. Oceanside Police Department officers who investigate the city's resident Crips and Bloods easily find well-produced, self-promoting songs and videos featuring local gang members on Internet web sites.

Gang Members in the Military

Members of nearly every major street gang as well as some prison gangs and OMGs have been identified on both domestic and international military installations. Deployments have resulted in gang members among service members and/or dependents on or near overseas bases. Additionally, military transfers have resulted in gang members, both service members and dependents/relatives, moving to new areas and establishing a gang presence.

Gang members with military training pose a unique threat to law enforcement personnel because of the distinctive military skills that they possess and their willingness to teach these skills to fellow gang members. While the number of gang members trained by the military is unknown, the threat that they pose to law enforcement is potentially significant, particularly if gang members trained in weapons, tactics, and planning pass this instruction on to other gang members. (See Table 1.) In addition, gang members currently serving in the military sometimes take advantage of their positions to engage in criminal activities such as trafficking weapons and drugs.

Table 1. Gangs Reported to Have Military-Trained Members

Gang Name	Type of Gang
18th Street	Gang Street
Aryan Brotherhood	Prison
Asian Boyz	Street
Bandidos	OMG
Black Disciples	Street
Bloods	Street
Crips	Street
Florencia 13	Street
Gangster Disciples	Street
Hells Angels	OMG
Latin Kings	Street
Mexican Mafia (La Eme)	Prison
Mongols	OMG
MS 13	Street
Norteños	Street
Outlaws Motorcycle Club	OMG
Sureños	Street
Vagos	OMG
Vice Lords	Street

Source: National Gang Intelligence Center.

Gang Relationship With DTOs and Other Criminal Organizations

Some larger gangs have developed regular working relationships with DTOs and other criminal organizations in Mexico, Central America, and Canada to develop sources of supply for wholesale quantities of illicit drugs and to facilitate other criminal activities. According to law enforcement information, gang members provide Mexican DTOs with support, such as smuggling, transportation, and security. Specific examples include:

- Some prison gangs are capable of directly controlling or influencing the smuggling of multihundred kilograms of cocaine and methamphetamine weekly into the United States.
- Texas-based, regional-level prison gangs cooperate with Mexico-based DTOs to smuggle wholesale quantities of cocaine and marijuana and illegal aliens into the United States from Mexico. Additionally, these gangs extort money from drug and alien traffickers transiting the Southwest Border.
- Some national-level Hispanic street gangs have close associations with Mexico-based DTOs. Hispanic gang members reportedly obtain cocaine and marijuana from the DTOs and transport the drugs to primary U.S. drug market areas for further distribution.
- Canada-based Chinese and Vietnamese DTOs and criminal groups maintain close working relationships with Asian gangs operating in Canada and the United States. Canada-based DTOs are the primary suppliers of multithousandtablet quantities of MDMA and multihundredpound quantities of high-potency marijuana to Asian gangs operating in the United States. The DTOs also use Asian gang members for other aspects of drug distribution operations in the United States.

Cross-Border Gang Activity

U.S.-based gang members are increasingly involved in cross-border criminal activities, particularly in areas of Texas and California along the U.S.–Mexico border. Much of this activity involves the trafficking of drugs and illegal aliens from Mexico into the United States and considerably adds to gang revenues. Further, gangs are increasingly smuggling weapons from the United States into Mexico as payment for drugs or to sell for a significant profit. Examples of such cross border activities include:

- Street and prison gang members have established networks that work closely with Mexican DTOs in trafficking cocaine and marijuana from Mexico into the United States for distribution.
- Some Mexican DTOs contract with gangs in the Southwest Region to smuggle weapons from the United States to Mexico, according to open source information.
- Street gang and OMG members are trafficking cocaine and firearms from the United States to Canada and marijuana and MDMA from Canada to the United States; this is a growing concern to U.S. and Canadian law enforcement

officials, particularly as Canadian law enforcement officials report that street gang-related gun crimes in Canada are often committed using firearms that are illegally smuggled into the country from the United States.

Gang Activity in Indian Country

Most street gangs active on reservations are local gangs, typically composed of Native American youth. Many of these local gangs have little or no direct ties to national-level street gangs; however, several Native American gangs, specifically Native Mob, have expanded beyond Indian Country on and off the reservations. Native Mob is one of the largest and most violent Native American street gangs operating in the United States. Native Mob is most active in Minnesota, Michigan, Wisconsin, North Dakota, and South Dakota. The main source of income for the gang is the retail-level distribution of illicit drugs, primarily marijuana and methamphetamine. Gang members also commit other crimes such as auto theft, assault, carjacking, drive-by shootings, extortion, homicide, and robbery.

Some urban and suburban gangs are expanding their drug operations onto Native American reservations. These gangs pose a significant threat to Indian Country because of their drug distribution activities and violent tendencies as well as the disruptive effect that they have on Native American communities. Gang members occasionally are employed by or work in conjunction with Mexican DTOs and criminal groups to distribute illicit drugs within Native American communities.

Female Involvement in Gangs

Female involvement in gangs continues to increase and evolve as females assume greater responsibility in gang activities and grow more independent from their male counterparts. Though gangs are still primarily male-dominated, research indicates that female gang membership is on the rise. In 2006 the National Youth Gang Center stated that "youth gang membership among girls has been more widely reported by law enforcement than in the past." In May 2008 the Office of Juvenile Justice and Delinquency Prevention (OJJDP) found that in high-risk, high-crime neighborhoods, 29.4 percent of girls and 32.4 percent of boys claimed gang membership when self-definition was used as a measure. The majority of respondents to a 2007 Florida-based study reported that female gang members accounted for less than 15 percent of gang members. However, a small portion of respondents placed female gang membership as high as 26 to 50 percent. In concurrence with each of the above studies, the National Council on Crime and Delinquency ranked "young females as the fastest growing offenders in the national juvenile justice population."

Although female gang membership in male-dominated gangs is increasing, the prevalence of predominantly female gangs continues to be a rare phenomenon. In addition, although all-female gangs do exist, they are infrequently the focus of law enforcement. Traditionally, female gangs have received less attention from researchers and law enforcement, and most efforts have focused on intervention programs designed to provide an alternative refuge for girls attempting to escape abusive environments. Furthermore, law enforcement officials are less likely to recognize or stop female gang members, and they have experienced difficulty in identifying female involvement in gang-related activity.

OUTLOOK

Most regions in the United States will experience increased gang membership, continued migration of gangs to suburban and rural areas, and increased gang-related criminal activity. These increases are largely the result of the continued expansion of gang-operated criminal networks. Better-organized urban gangs will continue to expand their criminal networks into new market areas in suburban and rural locations, where they can absorb unaffiliated local gangs or use violence to intimidate them.

Gang-related violence is very likely to remain at high levels or increase as gangs expand their criminal operations into suburban and rural communities. As these gangs encounter resistance from local gangs or other drug distributors in these communities, an increase in violent incidents such as assaults, drive-by shootings, and homicides can be expected.

Neighborhood-based gangs account for the majority of gangs active in the United States; however, national gangs commit more organized criminal activity and continue to expand their networks. Neighborhood-based gangs will continue to consume the resources of local law enforcement in communities that report high levels of gang-related criminal activity, but migration of national gangs into new areas will pose an increasing threat to such communities.

As gangs continue to expand and evolve from local- or regional-level gangs to sophisticated national-level gangs, most will continue to foster relationships with wholesale-level drug traffickers in Mexico and/or Canada. Such relationships are more likely for Hispanic gangs operating along the U.S.–Mexico border; these gang members often have personal and family ties to DTO members in Mexico.

Regional Summaries

The dynamics of gang activity vary significantly in each of the seven NGIC/GangTECC regions. (See Figure 1 on page 1.) The following regional summaries, organized alphabetically, provide overviews of the current gang situation in each region, highlighting major issues of concern to law enforcement

Central Region

More than 5,800 gangs with approximately 222,400 members are criminally active in the Central Region, according to NDTS 2008 data and interviews with local law enforcement officials. (See Figure 5.) Also according to NDTS data, the percentage of state and local law enforcement agencies in the Central Region that report gang activity in their jurisdictions increased from 45 percent in 2004 to 55 percent in 2008. Gangs are responsible for as much as 50 percent of the crime in some locations, according to local law enforcement officials. The most significant gangs operating in the Central Region are Chicago-based Gangster Disciples, Latin Kings, Vice Lords, and Black P. Stones. (See Appendix B.)

Gang-related trends:

- Gangs, particularly those with younger gang members, are responsible for an increasing percentage of crime in the region.
- Hispanic gangs in the Central Region are assuming a larger role in wholesale drug distribution.

Predictive NGIC/NDIC intelligence:

- As West Coast-based Hispanic gangs, particularly southern California-based Sureños 13 gangs, expand their presence in the Central Region,[6] gang-related violence associated with drug distribution territories very likely will increase.
- Chicago-based gangs will continue to dominate retail-level drug distribution in most urban areas of the Central Region.
- Chicago-based gangs will expand their presence in more suburban areas in the Central Region as a result of gang member migration from urban to suburban areas.
- Chicago-based gangs will develop direct access to drug sources of supply in Mexico.

6. Gang migration from California to other areas of the country may also be the result of the three strikes law in California.

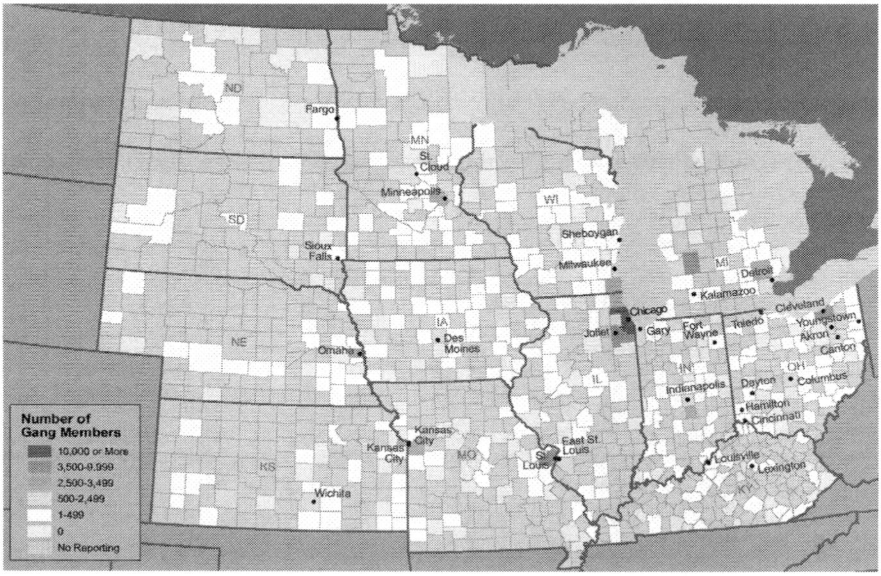

Figure 5. Central Region gang membership by county.

EAST REGION

More than 2,900 gangs with approximately 73,650 members are criminally active in the East Region, according to NDTS 2008 data and interviews with local law enforcement officials. (See Figure 6.) Also according to NDTS data, the percentage of state and local law enforcement agencies in the East Region that reported gang activity in their jurisdictions increased from 37 percent in 2004 to 57 percent in 2008. The most significant gangs operating in the East Region are Crips, Latin Kings, MS 13, Ñeta, and UBN.[7](See Appendix B.)

Gang-related trends:

- UBN is proliferating and expanding its influence over previously unaffiliated local gangs.
- Trinitarios[8], a Dominican street gang, is increasing its presence in the region.
- Over the past few years, MS 13 has posed a significant concern to law enforcement in the region, particularly in Maryland and Virginia. However, recent law enforcement actions against MS 13 members may have disrupted some of the gang's operations.

7. United Blood Nation (UBN) is a loose confederation of street gangs that formed in the Rikers Island Jail in New York City in 1993 and spread throughout the East Coast of the United States. It is one of the largest street gangs that follow the Bloods gang culture.

8. Trinitarios (meaning the Trinity or Special One) street gang was formed as a protection gang for Dominican inmates in New York prisons during the early 1990s. Upon leaving prison, members banded together as a street gang, calling themselves Trinitarians/ Trinitarios to separate the gang from other Dominican street gangs in New York. Trinitarios members are estab-lishing a reputation for extreme violence throughout the area.

- Gang-related violence has increased in many larger cities in the region.

Predictive NGIC/NDIC intelligence:

- National-level gangs, specifically Bloods gangs, and regional-level street gangs increasingly will attempt to influence and control local gangs, resulting in an escalation of gang-related violence in the East Region.
- Gangs in the East Region very likely will continue to expand their operations from urban communities into suburban and rural locations throughout the region and into the Southeast, New England, and Central Regions.

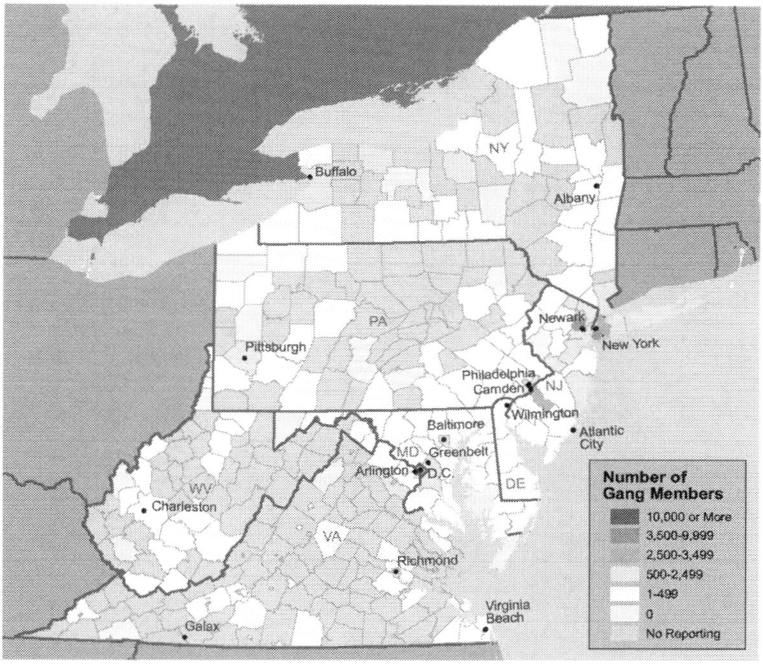

Figure 6. East Region gang membership by county.

NEW ENGLAND REGION

Approximately 640 gangs with more than 17,250 members are criminally active in the New England Region, according to 2008 NDTS data and local law enforcement reporting. (See Figure 7.) Also according to NDTS data, the percentage of state and local law enforcement agencies in the New England Region that report gang activity in their jurisdictions increased from 28 percent in 2004 to 39 percent in 2008. Gangs are responsible for as much as 60 percent of the crime in some communities. The most significant gangs operating in the New England Region are Hells Angels, Latin Kings, Outlaws, Tiny Rascal Gangster Crips, and UBN. (See Appendices B and D.)

Gang-related trends:

- Trinitarios are an emerging gang in the region.
- Sureños 13 gang activity is increasing.
- Gang-related violence is increasing as a result of competition among gangs for control of territories.
- African American, Asian, and Hispanic gang members often use violence to gain control over the retail-level and midlevel distribution of cocaine, heroin, and marijuana in many locations, according to local and federal law enforcement information. For example, violence between Bloods and Crips members recently has escalated as a direct result of a conflict between the gangs for control of retail-level drug distribution.
- The number of gangs associating with DTOs is growing.

Predictive NGIC/NDIC intelligence:

- Criminal activity related to street gangs likely will increase throughout the New England Region. Armed robberies, carjackings, drug trafficking, extortions, and home invasions are likely to increase because of the influx of Bloods, Crips, Latin Kings, and Trinitarios members from neighboring regions.

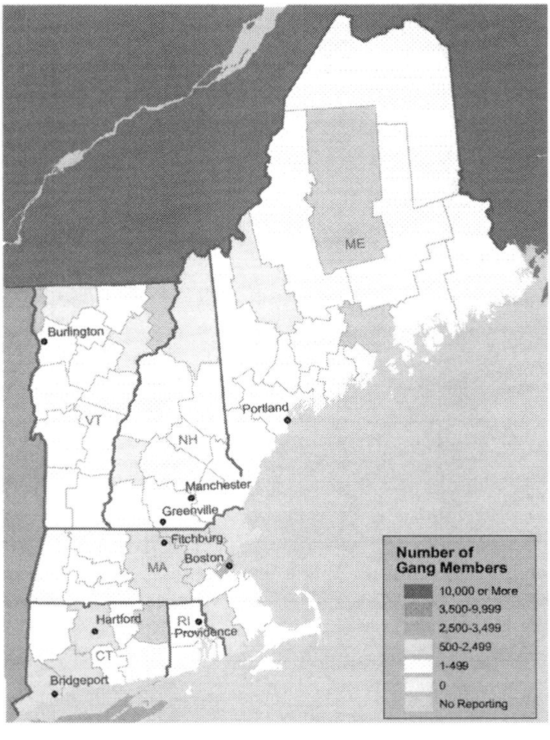

Figure 7. New England Region gang membership by county.

Northwest Region

Approximately 2,093 gangs with more than 36,650 members are criminally active in the Northwest Region, according to 2008 NDTS data and interviews with local law enforcement officials. (See Figure 8.) Also according to NDTS data, the percentage of state and local law enforcement agencies in the Northwest Region that report gang activity in their jurisdictions has increased from 46 percent in 2004 to 58 percent in 2008. Gang members are responsible for as much as 80 percent of violent crime in some communities in region. The most significant gangs operating in the Northwest Region are Bloods, Crips (74 Hoover and Rolling 60s), Gangster Disciples, Norteños, and Sureños gangs, including Brown Pride, Florencia 13, and Varrio Locos 13. (See Appendix B.)

Gang-related trends:

- Hispanic gangs aligned with the California-based La Eme have migrated into the Northwest Region. other to survive.
- Conflicts between the relocated California-based Hispanic gangs and local African American and Hispanic gangs have resulted in increased violence.

Predictive NGIC/NDIC intelligence:

- As gang-related violence escalates, smaller gangs likely will merge or align with one an-other to survive.
- Alliances between gangs may result in the expansion of criminal networks and increased criminal activity in the Northwest Region.

Figure 8. Northwest Region gang membership by county

Pacific Region

Approximately 6,900 gangs with more than 237,000 members are criminally active in the Pacific Region, according to 2008 NDTS data and interviews with local law enforcement officials. (See Figure 9.) Also according to NDTS data, the percentage of state and local law enforcement agencies in the Pacific Region that report gang activity in their jurisdictions increased from 66 percent in 2004 to 74 percent in 2008. As much as 80 percent of crime in some jurisdictions is gang-related, according to law enforcement reporting. The most significant gangs operating in the Pacific Region are 18th Street, Bloods, Crips, La Eme, Nuestra Familia, and Hells Angels. (See Appendices B and D.)

Gang-related trends:

- MS 13 poses a significant threat to local law enforcement. The gang is involved in criminal activities including drug trafficking, extortion, and firearms violations.

Predictive NGIC/NDIC intelligence:

- Hispanic gangs, specifically 18th Street, La Eme, Nuestra Familia, and MS 13, will continue to fight for control of retail-level drug distribution in locations throughout the Pacific Region.

- Gang-related criminal activity in the Pacific Region is significant and likely will remain significant as gang members continue to fight for control of territories.
- Gang-related extortion and firearms violations likely will increase.

Figure 9. Pacific Region gang membership by county.

Southeast Region

Approximately 9,871 gangs with more than 172,360 members are criminally active in the Southeast Region, according to 2008 NDTS data and interviews with local law enforcement officials. (See Figure 10.) Also according to NDTS data, the percentage of state and local law enforcement agencies in the Southeast Region that report gang activity in their jurisdictions has increased from 50 percent in 2004 to 68 percent in 2008. The most significant gangs operating in the region are Crips, Gangster Disciples, Latin Kings, Sureños 13, and UBN. (See Appendix B.)

Gang-related trends:

- The presence of MS 13 in North Carolina and Georgia is growing.
- The increased migration of Hispanic gangs into the region has resulted in violent confrontations with local African American gangs for control of gang territories.
- Mexican DTOs have increased their criminal operations in the region over the past few years, providing gangs, particularly Hispanic gangs, in the region with a steady supply of drugs that they have used to expand their drug distribution operations.

Predictive NGIC/NDIC intelligence:

- Hispanic gangs will expand their drug distribution operations in the Southeast Region.
- Hispanic gangs will establish more direct associations with Mexican sources of supply for drugs.
- Hispanic gangs will take a more active role in developing independent transportation and distribution networks in the region.
- Some Hispanic gangs in the Southeast Region will transition from retail-level drug sales to wholesale-level distribution, which may lead to violent confrontations with other wholesale drug distributors in the region.

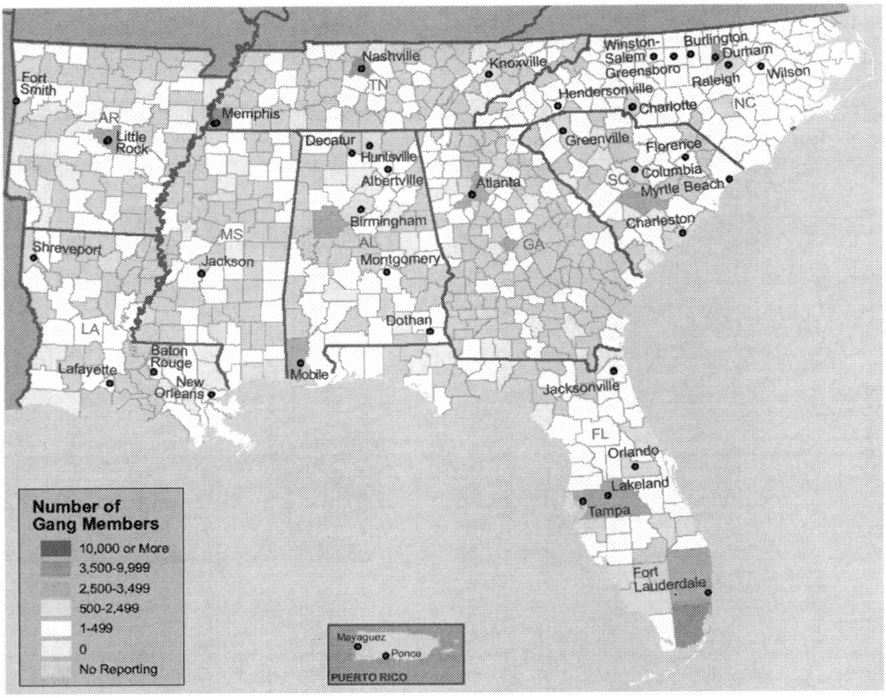

Figure 10. Southeast Region gang membership by county.

Southwest Region

Approximately 5,297 gangs with nearly 111,000 members are criminally active in the Southwest Region, according to 2008 NDTS data and local law enforcement reporting. (See Figure 11.) Also according to NDTS data, the percentage of state and local law enforcement agencies in the Southwest Region that report gang activity in their jurisdictions increased from 52 percent in 2004 to 63 percent in 2008. According to interviews with local law enforcement officers, gangs are responsible for as much as 60 percent of crime in some communities in the Southwest Region. The most significant gangs operating in the region are Barrio Azteca, Latin Kings, Mexikanemi, Tango Blast, and Texas Syndicate. (See Appendices B and C.)

Gang-related trends:

- Gangs are increasingly conducting cross-border criminal activities such as the trafficking of illegal aliens and drugs from Mexico into the United States.
- Many gangs have established sets in Mexico and maintain associations with local DTOs and Mexican DTO representatives.
- A number of gangs in the Southwest Region are smuggling firearms from the United States into Mexico as payment for drugs or to sell for a significant profit.

Predictive NGIC/NDIC intelligence:

- Prison and street gangs in the Southwest Region will continue to develop and strengthen their ties to Mexican DTOs. Mexican DTOs may allow gangs to assume a larger role in wholesale drug smuggling across the U.S.– Mexico border and in wholesale distribution within the Southwest Region. Doing so would reduce the risks that Mexican DTOs face from U.S. law enforcement.

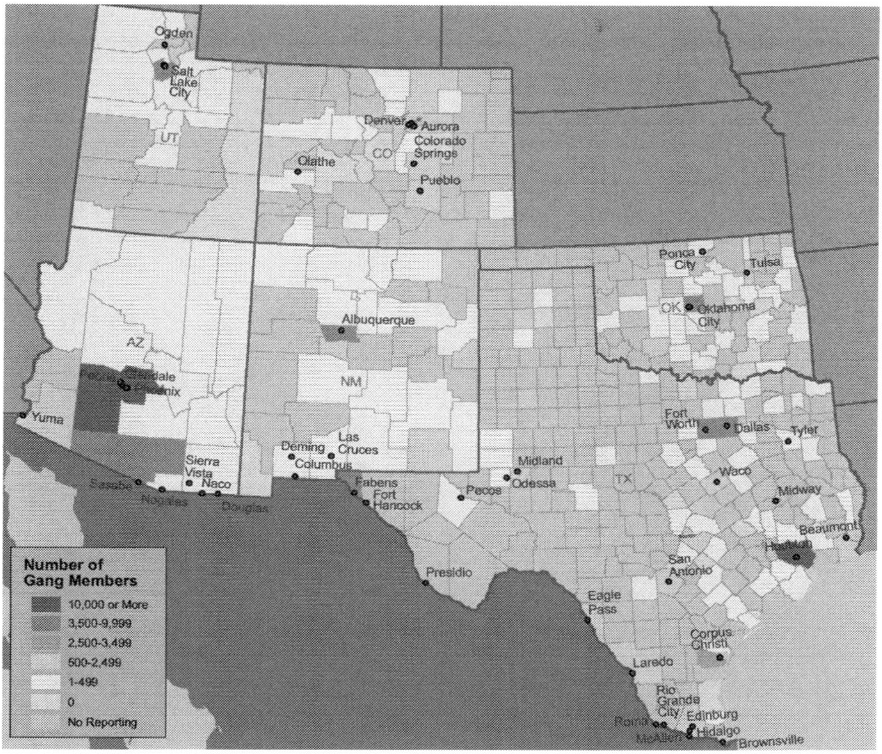

Figure 11. Southwest Region gang membership by county.

Appendix A. Maps

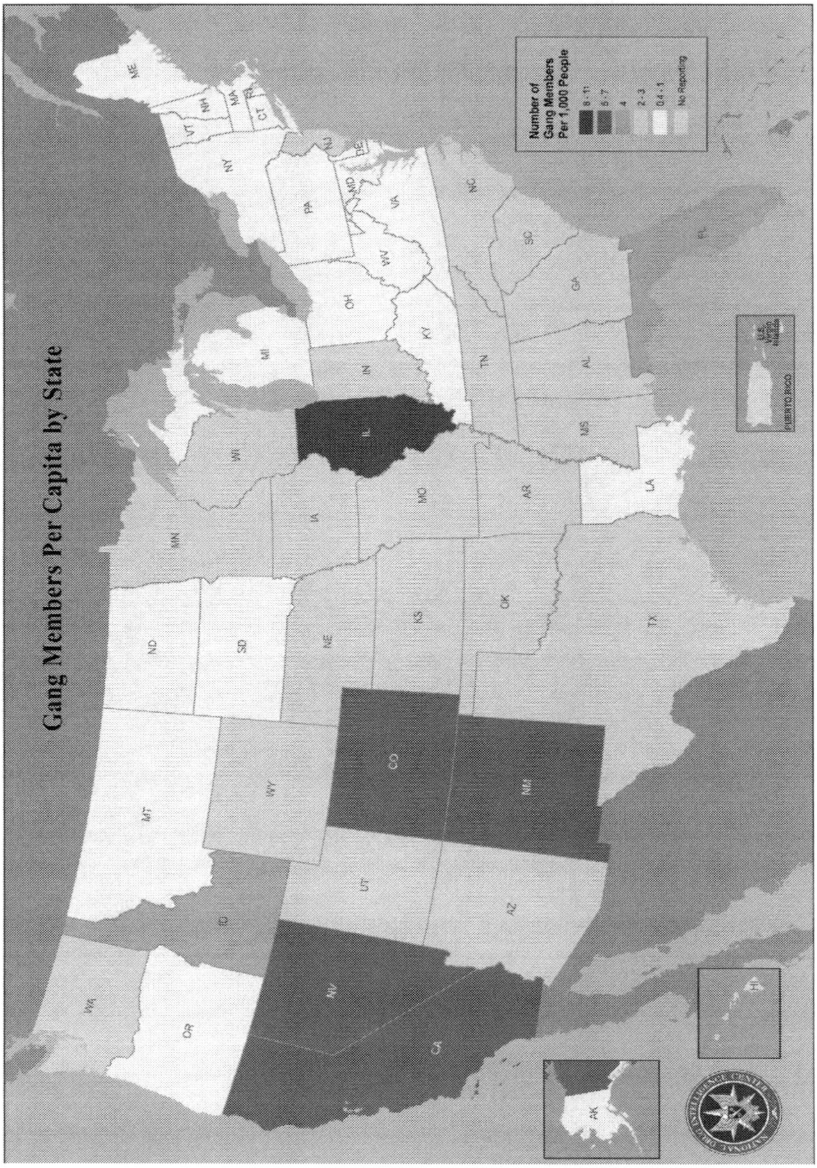

Map 1. Gang membership per capita, by state.

Source: National Drug Threat Survey 2008; field program specialist field surveys of state and local law enforcement 2008; and U.S. Census population estimates 2006.

Appendix B. Street Gangs

18th Street (National)

Formed in Los Angeles, 18th Street is a group of loosely associated sets or cliques, each led by an influential member. Membership is estimated at 30,000 to 50,000. In California approximately 80 percent of the gang's members are illegal aliens from Mexico and Central America. The gang is active in 44 cities in 20 states. Its main source of income is street-level distribution of cocaine and marijuana and, to a lesser extent, heroin and methamphetamine. Gang members also commit assault, auto theft, carjacking, drive-by shootings, extortion, homicide, identification fraud, and robbery.

Almighty Latin King and Queen Nation (National)

The Latin Kings street gang was formed in Chicago in the 1960s and consisted predominantly of Mexican and Puerto Rican males. Originally created with the philosophy of overcoming racial prejudice and creating an organization of "Kings," the Latin Kings evolved into a criminal enterprise operating throughout the United States under two umbrella factions—Motherland, also known as KMC (King Motherland Chicago), and Bloodline (New York). All members of the gang refer to themselves as Latin Kings and, currently, individuals of any nationality are allowed to become members. Latin Kings associating with the Motherland faction also identify themselves as "Almighty Latin King Nation (ALKN)," and make up more than 160 structured chapters operating in 158 cities in 31 states. The membership of Latin Kings following KMC is estimated to be 20,000 to 35,000. The Bloodline was founded by Luis Felipe in the New York State correctional system in 1986. Latin Kings associating with Bloodline also identify themselves as the "Almighty Latin King and Queen Nation (ALKQN)." Membership is estimated to be 2,200 to 7,500, divided among several dozen chapters operating in 15 cities in 5 states. Bloodline Latin Kings share a common culture and structure with KMC and respect them as the Motherland, but all chapters do not report to the Chicago leadership hierarchy. The gang's primary source of income is the street-level distribution of powder cocaine, crack cocaine, heroin, and marijuana. Latin Kings continue to portray themselves as a community organization while engaging in a wide variety of criminal activities, including assault, burglary, homicide, identity theft, and money laundering.

Asian Boyz (National)

Asian Boyz is one of the largest Asian street gangs operating in the United States. Formed in southern California in the early 1970s, the gang is estimated to have 1,300 to 2,000 members operating in at least 28 cities in 14 states. Members primarily are Vietnamese or Cambodian males. Members of Asian Boyz are involved in producing, transporting, and distributing methamphetamine as well as distributing MDMA and marijuana. In addition, gang members are involved in other criminal activities, including assault, burglary, drive-by shootings, and homicide.

Black P. Stone Nation (National)

Black P. Stone Nation, one of the largest and most violent associations of street gangs in the United States, consists of seven highly structured street gangs with a single leader and a common culture. It has an estimated 6,000 to 8,000 members, most of whom are African American males from the Chicago metropolitan area. The gang's main source of income is the street-level distribution of cocaine, heroin, marijuana and, to a lesser extent, methamphetamine. Members also are involved in many other types of criminal activity, including assault, auto theft, burglary, carjacking, drive-by shootings, extortion, homicide, and robbery.

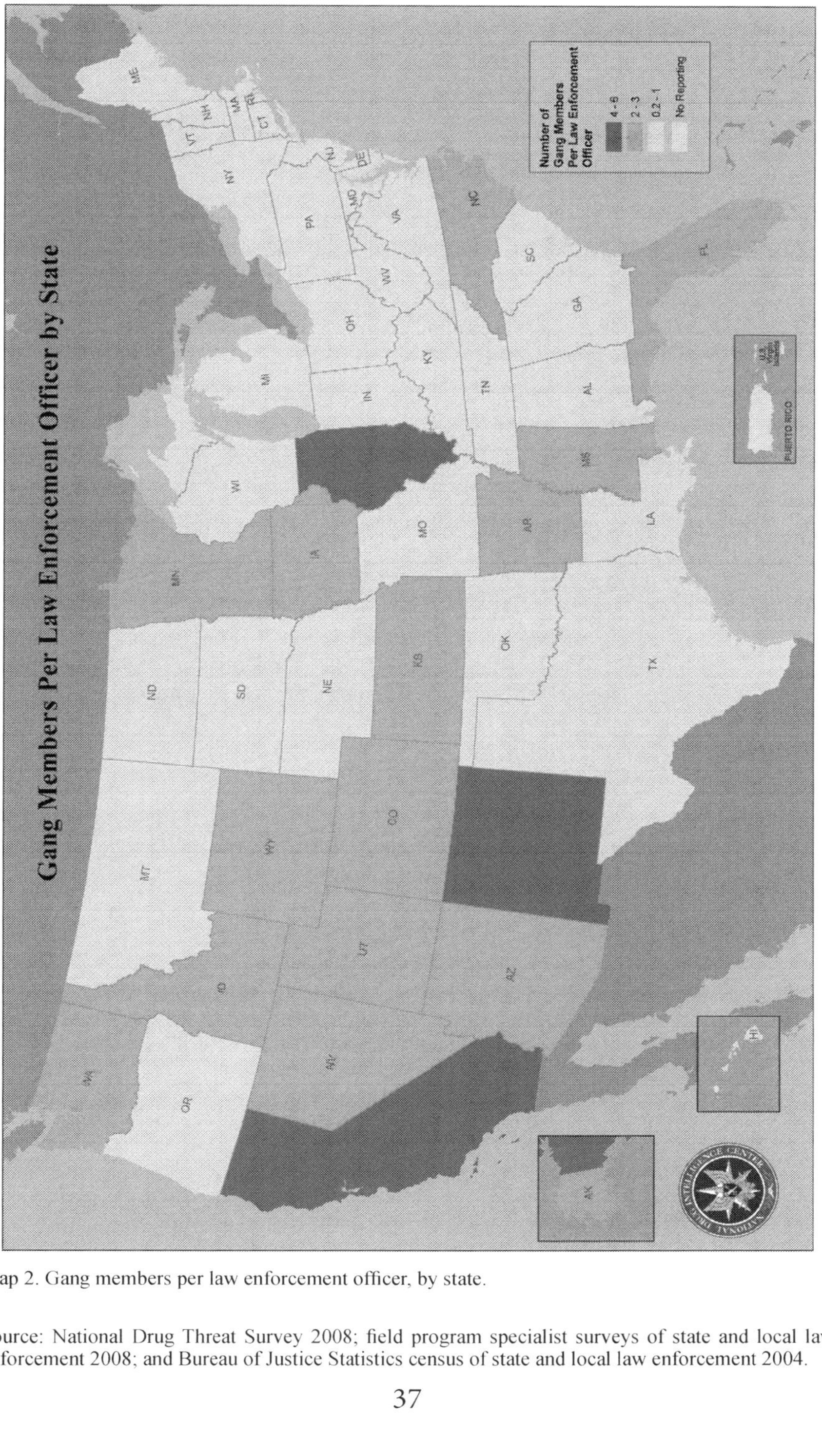

Map 2. Gang members per law enforcement officer, by state.

Source: National Drug Threat Survey 2008; field program specialist surveys of state and local law enforcement 2008; and Bureau of Justice Statistics census of state and local law enforcement 2004.

Bloods (National)

Bloods is an association of structured and unstructured gangs that have adopted a single-gang culture. The original Bloods were formed in the early 1970s to provide protection from the Crips street gang in Los Angeles, California. Large, national-level Bloods gangs include Bounty Hunter Bloods and Crenshaw Mafia Gangsters. Bloods membership is estimated to be 7,000 to 30,000 nationwide; most members are African American males. Bloods gangs are active in 123 cities in 33 states. The main source of income for Bloods gangs is street-level distribution of cocaine and marijuana. Bloods members also are involved in transporting and distributing methamphetamine, heroin, and PCP (phencyclidine), but to a much lesser extent. The gangs also are involved in other criminal activity including assault, auto theft, burglary, carjacking, drive-by shootings, extortion, homicide, identity fraud, and robbery.

Crips (National)

Crips is a collection of structured and unstructured gangs that have adopted a common gang culture. Crips membership is estimated at 30,000 to 35,000; most members are African American males from the Los Angeles metropolitan area. Large, national-level Crips gangs include 107 Hoover Crips, Insane Gangster Crips, and Rolling 60s Crips. Crips gangs operate in 221 cities in 41 states. The main source of income for Crips gangs is the street-level distribution of powder cocaine, crack cocaine, marijuana, and PCP. The gangs also are involved in other criminal activity such as assault, auto theft, burglary, and homicide.

Florencia 13 (Regional)

Florencia 13 (F 13 or FX 13) originated in Los Angeles in the early 1960s; gang membership is estimated at more than 3,000 members. The gang operates primarily in California and increasingly in Arkansas, Missouri, New Mexico, and Utah. Florencia 13 is subordinate to the Mexican Mafia (La Eme) prison gang and claims Sureños (Sur 13) affiliation. A primary source of income for gang members is the trafficking of cocaine and methamphetamine. Gang members smuggle multikilogram quantities of powder cocaine and methamphetamine obtained from supply sources in Mexico into the United States for distribution. Also, gang members produce large quantities of methamphetamine in southern California for local distribution. Florencia members are involved in other criminal activities, including assault, drive-by shootings, and homicide.

Fresno Bulldogs (Regional)

Fresno Bulldogs is a street gang that originated in Fresno, California, in the late 1960s. Bulldogs is the largest Hispanic gang operating in central California, with membership estimated at 5,000 to 6,000. Bulldogs is one of the few Hispanic gangs in California that claim neither Sureños (Southern) nor Norteños (Northern) affiliation. However, gang members associate with Nuestra Familia (NF) members, particularly when trafficking drugs. The street-level distribution of methamphetamine, marijuana, and heroin is a primary source of income for gang members. In addition, members are involved in other criminal activity, including assault, burglary, homicide, and robbery.

Gangster Disciples (National)

The Gangster Disciples street gang was formed in Chicago, Illinois, in the mid-1960s. It is structured like a corporation and is led by a chairman of the board. Gang membership is estimated at 25,000 to 50,000; most members are African American males from the Chicago metropolitan area. The gang is active in 110 cities in 31 states. Its main source of income is the street-level distribution of cocaine, crack cocaine, marijuana, and heroin. The gang also is involved in other criminal activity, including assault, auto theft, firearms violations, fraud, homicide, the operation of prostitution rings, and money laundering.

Latin Disciples (Regional)

Latin Disciples, also known as Maniac Latin Disciples and Young Latino Organization, originated in Chicago in the late 1960s. The gang is composed of at least 10 structured and unstructured factions with an estimated 1,500 to 2,000 members and associate members. Most members are Puerto Rican males. Maniac Latin Disciples is the largest Hispanic gang in the Folk Nation Alliance. The gang is most active in the Great Lakes and southwestern regions of the United States. The street-level distribution of powder cocaine, heroin, marijuana, and PCP is a primary source of income for the gang. Members also are involved in other criminal activity, including assault, auto theft, carjacking, drive-by shootings, home invasion, homicide, money laundering, and weapons trafficking.

Mara Salvatrucha (National)

Mara Salvatrucha, also known as MS 13, is one of the largest Hispanic street gangs in the United States. Traditionally, the gang consisted of loosely affiliated groups known as cliques; however, law enforcement officials have reported increased coordination of criminal activity among Mara Salvatrucha cliques in the Atlanta, Dallas, Los Angeles, Washington, D.C., and New York metropolitan areas. The gang is estimated to have 30,000 to 50,000 members and associate members worldwide, 8,000 to 10,000 of whom reside in the United States. Members smuggle illicit drugs, primarily powder cocaine and marijuana, into the United States and transport and distribute the drugs throughout the country. Some members also are involved in alien smuggling, assault, drive-by shootings, homicide, identity theft, prostitution operations, robbery, and weapons trafficking.

Sureños and Norteños (National)

As individual Hispanic street gang members enter prison systems, they put aside former rivalries with other Hispanic street gangs and unite under the name Sureños or Norteños. The original Mexican Mafia members, most of whom were from southern California, considered Mexicans from the rural, agricultural areas of northern California weak and viewed them with contempt. To distinguish themselves from the agricultural workers or farmers from northern California, members of Mexican Mafia began to refer to the Hispanic gang members who worked for them as Sureños (Southerners). Inmates from northern California became known as Norteños (Northerners) and are affiliated with Nuestra Familia. Because of its size and strength, Fresno Bulldogs is the only Hispanic gang in the California Department of Corrections (CDC) that does not fall under Sureños or Norteños but remains independent. Sureños gang members' main sources of income are retail-level distribution of cocaine, heroin, marijuana, and methamphetamine within prison systems and in the community as well as extortion of drug distributors on the streets. Some members have direct links to Mexican DTOs and broker deals for Mexican Mafia as well as their own gang. Sureños gangs also are involved in other criminal activities such as assault, carjacking, home invasion, homicide, and robbery. Norteños gang members' main sources of income are the retail-level distribution of cocaine, heroin, marijuana, methamphetamine, and PCP within prison systems and in the community as well as extortion of drug distributors on the streets. Norteños gangs also are involved in other criminal activities such as assault, carjacking, home invasion, homicide, and robbery.

Tango Blast (Regional)

Tango Blast is one of largest prison/street criminal gangs operating in Texas. Tango Blast's criminal activities include drug trafficking, extortion, kidnapping, sexual assault, and murder. In the late 1990s, Hispanic men incarcerated in federal, state, and local prisons founded Tango Blast for personal protection against violence from traditional prison gangs such as the Aryan Brotherhood, Texas Syndicate, and Texas Mexican Mafia. Tango Blast originally had four city-based chapters: Houstone, Houston, Texas; ATX or La Capricha, Austin, Texas; D-Town, Dallas, Texas; and Foros or Foritos, Fort Worth, Texas. These founding four chapters are collectively known as Puro Tango Blast or the Four Horsemen. From the original four chapters, former Texas inmates established new chapters in El Paso, San Antonio, Corpus Christi, and the Rio Grande Valley. In June 2008 the Houston Police Department (HPD) estimated that more than 14,000 Tango Blast members were incarcerated in Texas. Tango Blast is difficult to monitor. The gang does not conform to either traditional prison/street gang hierarchical organization or gang rules. Tango Blast is laterally organized, and leaders are elected sporadically to represent the gang in prisons and to lead street gang cells. The significance of Tango Blast is exemplified by corrections officials reporting that rival traditional prison gangs are now forming alliances to defend themselves against Tango Blast's growing power.

Tiny Rascal Gangsters (National)

Tiny Rascal Gangsters is one of the largest and most violent Asian street gang associations in the United States. It is composed of at least 60 structured and unstructured gangs, commonly referred to as sets, with an estimated 5,000 to 10,000 members and associates who have adopted a common gang culture. Most members are Asian American males. The sets are most active in the southwestern, Pacific, and New England regions of the United States. The street-level distribution of powder cocaine, marijuana, MDMA, and methamphetamine is a primary source of income for the sets. Members also are involved in other criminal activity, including assault, drive-by shootings, extortion, home invasion, homicide, robbery, and theft.

United Blood Nation (Regional)

Bloods is a universal term that is used to identify both West Coast Bloods and United Blood Nation (UBN). While these groups are traditionally distinct entities, both identify themselves by "Blood," often making it hard for law enforcement to distinguish between them. United Blood Nation (UBN) started in 1993 in Rikers Island GMDC (George Mochen Detention Center) to form protection from the threat posed by Latin Kings and Ñetas, who dominated the prison. United Blood Nation (UBN) is a loose confederation of street gangs, or sets, that once were predominantly African American. Membership is estimated to be between 7,000 and 15,000 along the U.S. eastern corridor. UBN derives its income from street-level distribution of cocaine, heroin, and marijuana; robbery; auto theft; and smuggling drugs to prison inmates. UBN members also engage in arson, carjacking, credit card fraud, extortion, homicide, identity theft, intimidation, prostitution operations, and weapons distribution.

Vice Lord Nation (National)

Vice Lord Nation, based in Chicago, is a collection of structured gangs located in 74 cities in 28 states, primarily in the Great Lakes region. Led by a national board, the various gangs have an estimated 30,000 to 35,000 members, most of whom are African American males. The main source of income is street-level distribution of cocaine, heroin, and marijuana. Members also engage in other criminal activity such as assault, burglary, homicide, identity theft, and money laundering.

Appendix C. Prison Gangs

Aryan Brotherhood

Aryan Brotherhood, also known as AB, was originally ruled by consensus but is now highly structured with two factions—one in the CDC and the other in the Federal Bureau of Prisons (BOP). The majority of members are Caucasian males, and the gang is active primarily in the southwestern and Pacific regions. Its main source of income is the distribution of cocaine, heroin, marijuana, and methamphetamine within prison systems and on the streets. Some AB members have business relationships with Mexican DTOs that smuggle illegal drugs into California for AB distribution. AB is notoriously violent and is often involved in murder for hire. Although the gang has been historically linked to the California-based Hispanic prison gang Mexican Mafia (La Eme), tension between AB and La Eme is increasingly evident, as seen in recent fights between Caucasians and Hispanics within CDC.

Barrio Azteca

Barrio Azteca is one of the most violent prison gangs in the United States. The gang is highly structured and has an estimated membership of 2,000. Most members are Mexican national or Mexican American males. Barrio Azteca is most active in the southwestern region, primarily in federal, state, and local corrections facilities in Texas and outside prison in southwestern Texas and southeastern New Mexico. The gang's main source of income is derived from smuggling heroin, powder cocaine, and marijuana from Mexico into the United States for distribution both inside and outside prisons. Gang members often transport illicit drugs across the U.S.–Mexico border for DTOs. Barrio Azteca members also are involved in alien smuggling, arson, assault, auto theft, burglary, extortion, intimidation, kidnapping, robbery, and weapons violations.

Black Guerrilla Family

Black Guerrilla Family (BGF), originally called Black Family or Black Vanguard, is a prison gang founded in the San Quentin State Prison, California, in 1966. The gang is highly organized along paramilitary lines, with a supreme leader and central committee. BGF has an established national charter, code of ethics, and oath of allegiance. BGF members operate primarily in California and Maryland. The gang has 100 to 300 members, most of whom are African American males. A primary source of income for gang members comes from cocaine and marijuana distribution. BGF members obtain such drugs primarily from Nuestra Familia/Norteños members or from local Mexican traffickers. BGF members are involved in other criminal activities, including auto theft, burglary, drive-by shootings, and homicide.

Hermanos de Pistoleros Latinos

Hermanos de Pistoleros Latinos (HPL) is a Hispanic prison gang formed in the Texas Department of Criminal Justice (TDCJ) in the late 1980s. It operates in most prisons and on the streets in many communities in Texas, particularly Laredo. HPL is also active in several cities in Mexico, and its largest contingent in that country is in Nuevo Laredo. The gang is structured and is estimated to have 1,000 members. Members maintain close ties to several Mexican DTOs and are involved in trafficking quantities of cocaine and marijuana from Mexico into the United States for distribution.

Mexikanemi

The Mexikanemi prison gang (also known as Texas Mexican Mafia or Emi) was formed in the early 1980s within the Texas Department of Criminal Justice (TDCJ). The gang is highly structured and is estimated to have 2,000 members, most of whom are Mexican nationals or Mexican American males living in Texas at the time of incarceration. Mexikanemi poses a significant drug trafficking threat to communities in the southwestern United States, particularly in Texas. Gang members reportedly traffic multikilogram quantities of powder cocaine, heroin, and methamphetamine; multiton quantities of marijuana; and thousand-tablet quantities of MDMA from Mexico into the United States for distribution inside and outside prison. Gang members obtain drugs from associates or members of the Jaime Herrera-Herrera, Osiel Cárdenas-Guillén, and/or Vicente Carrillo-Fuentes Mexican DTOs. In addition, Mexikanemi members maintain a relationship with Los Zetas, a Mexican paramilitary/criminal organization employed by the Cárdenas-Guillén DTO as its personal security force.

Mexican Mafia

The Mexican Mafia prison gang, also known as La Eme (Spanish for the letter M), was formed in the late 1950s within the CDC. It is loosely structured and has strict rules that must be followed by the 200 members. Most members are Mexican American males who previously belonged to a southern California street gang. Mexican Mafia is primarily active in the southwestern and Pacific regions of the United States, but its power base is in California. The gang's main source of income is extorting drug distributors outside prison and distributing methamphetamine, cocaine, heroin, and marijuana within prison systems and on the streets. Some members have direct links to Mexican DTOs and broker deals for themselves and their associates. Mexican Mafia also is involved in other criminal activities, including controlling gambling and homosexual prostitution in prison.

Ñeta

Ñeta is a prison gang that began in Puerto Rico and spread to the United States. Ñeta is one of the largest and most violent prison gangs, with about 7,000 members in Puerto Rico and 5,000 in the United States. Ñeta chapters in Puerto Rico exist exclusively inside prisons; once members are released from prison they are no longer considered part of the gang. In the United States, Ñeta chapters exist inside and outside prisons in 36 cities in nine states, primarily in the Northeast. The gang's main source of income is retail distribution of powder and crack cocaine, heroin, marijuana and, to a lesser extent, LSD, MDMA, methamphetamine, and PCP. Ñeta members commit assault, auto theft, burglary, drive-by shootings, extortion, home invasion, money laundering, robbery, weapons and explosives trafficking, and witness intimidation.

Appendix D. Outlaw Motorcycle Gangs

Bandidos

Bandidos Motorcycle Club, an OMG with 2,000 to 2,500 members in the United States and 13 other countries, is a growing criminal threat to the nation. Law enforcement authorities estimate that Bandidos is one of the two largest OMGs in the United States, with approximately 900 members belonging to more than 88 chapters in 16 states. Bandidos is involved in transporting and distributing cocaine and marijuana and producing, transporting, and distributing methamphetamine. Bandidos is most active in the Pacific, southeastern, southwestern, and west central regions and is expanding in these regions by forming new chapters and allowing members of support clubs to form or join Bandidos chapters. The members of support clubs are known as "puppet" or "duck" club members. They do the dirty work of the mother club.

Hells Angels

Hells Angels Motorcycle Club (HAMC) is an OMG with 2,000 to 2,500 members belonging to more than 250 chapters in the United States and 26 foreign countries. HAMC poses a criminal threat on six continents. U.S. law enforcement authorities estimate that HAMC has more than 69 chapters in 22 states with 900 to 950 members. HAMC produces, transports, and distributes marijuana and methamphetamine and transports and distributes cocaine, hashish, heroin, LSD (lysergic acid diethylamide), MDMA, PCP, and diverted pharmaceuticals. HAMC is involved in other criminal activity, including assault, extortion, homicide, money laundering, and motorcycle theft.

Mongols

Mongols Motorcycle Club is an extremely violent OMG that poses a serious criminal threat to the Pacific and southwestern regions of the United States. Mongols members transport and distribute cocaine, marijuana, and methamphetamine and frequently commit violent crimes, including assault, intimidation, and murder, to defend Mongols territory and uphold its reputation. Mongols has 70 chapters nationwide, with most of the club's 800 to 850 members residing in California. Many members are former street gang members with a long history of using violence to settle grievances. Agents with the ATF have called Mongols Motorcycle Club the most violent and dangerous OMG in the nation. In the 1980s, the Mongols OMG seized control of southern California from HAMC, and today Mongols club is allied with Bandidos, Outlaws, Sons of Silence, and Pagan's OMGs against HAMC. The Mongols club also maintains ties to Hispanic street gangs in Los Angeles.

Outlaws

Outlaws Motorcycle Club has more than 1,700 members belonging to 176 chapters in the United States and 12 foreign countries. U.S. law enforcement authorities estimate that Outlaws has more than 94 chapters in 22 states with more than 700 members. Outlaws also identifies itself as the American Outlaws Association (A.O.A.) and Outlaws Nation. Outlaws is the dominant OMG in the Great Lakes region. Gang members produce, transport, and distribute methamphetamine and transport and distribute cocaine, marijuana and, to a lesser extent, MDMA. Outlaws members engage in various criminal activities, including arson, assault, explosives operations, extortion, fraud, homicide, intimidation, kidnapping, money laundering, prostitution operations, robbery, theft, and weapons violations. It competes with HAMC for membership and territory.

Sons of Silence

Sons of Silence Motorcycle Club (SOSMC) is one of the largest OMGs in the United States, with 250 to 275 members among 30 chapters in 12 states. The club also has five chapters in Germany. SOSMC members have been implicated in numerous criminal activities, including murder, assault, drug trafficking, intimidation, extortion, prostitution operations, money laundering, weapons trafficking, and motorcycle and motorcycle parts theft.

APPENDIX E. SOURCES

The sources of information used for this assessment are listed below. Numerous state and local law enforcement agencies throughout the United States provided valuable input to this report through their participation in the National Drug Threat Survey and interviews with NDIC Field Program Specialists. These agencies were too numerous to thank individually.

FEDERAL

Executive Office of the President
- Office of National Drug Control Policy
  - High Intensity Drug Trafficking Areas
    - Appalachia
    - Arizona
    - Atlanta
    - California Border Alliance Group
    - Central Florida
    - Central Valley California
    - Chicago
    - Gulf Coast
    - Hawaii
    - Houston
    - Lake County
    - Los Angeles
    - Michigan
    - Midwest
    - Milwaukee
    - Nevada
    - New England
    - New Mexico
    - New York/New Jersey
    - Northern California
    - North Florida
    - North Texas
    - Northwest
    - Ohio
    - Oregon
    - Philadelphia/Camden
    - Puerto Rico/U.S. Virgin Islands
    - Rocky Mountain

South Florida
South Texas
Washington/Baltimore
West Texas

U.S. Department of Defense
United States Army
Criminal Investigation Division

U.S. Department of Homeland Security
U.S. Customs and Border Protection

U.S. Department of Justice
Bureau of Alcohol, Tobacco, Firearms and Explosives
Criminal Division
Organized Crime Drug Enforcement Task Force
Drug Enforcement Administration
Boston/New England Field Division
Dallas Field Division
El Paso Intelligence Center
Houston Field Division
Philadelphia Field Division
San Diego Field Division
Seattle Field Division
Federal Bureau of Investigation
Atlanta Field Division
Boston Field Division
Buffalo Field Division
Chicago Field Division
Dallas Field Division
Kansas City Field Division
Los Angeles Field Division
New Haven Field Division
Philadelphia Field Division
Sacramento Field Division
Salt Lake City Field Division
San Diego Field Division
San Francisco Field Division
Seattle Field Division
St. Louis Field Division
Federal Bureau of Prisons
National Gang Intelligence Center
Office of Justice Programs
Bureau of Justice Assistance

Bureau of Justice Statistics

Local, State, and Regional

Alabama

Alabama Department of Corrections
Anniston Police Department
Birmingham Police Department
Decatur Police Department
Gadsden Police Department
Huntsville Police Department
Mobile Police Department
Montgomery Police Department
Tuscaloosa Police Department

Alaska

Alaska State Police
Anchorage Police Department
Fairbanks Police Department
Juneau Police Department
University of Alaska-Fairbanks
University Police Department

Arizona

Arizona Department of Corrections
Douglas Police Department
Glendale Police Department
Nogales Police Department
Phoenix Police Department
Tucson Police Department
Yuma Police Department

Arkansas

Fort Smith Police Department
Jonesboro Police Department
Little Rock Police Department
Rogers Police Department

California

Anaheim Police Department
Calexico Police Department
California Department of Corrections and Rehabilitation

California Department of Justice
    Bureau of Intelligence and Investigation
Campbell Police Department
Chula Vista Police Department
El Cajon Police Department
El Centro Police Department
Fresno County Sheriff's Office
Fresno Police Department
Glendale Police Department
Hayward Police Department
Humboldt County Sheriff's Office
Lake County Sheriff's Office
Los Angeles County Sheriff's Office
Los Angeles Police Department
Merced Police Department
Modesto Police Department
Moreno Valley Task Force
Napa Police Department
Oakland Police Department
Oceanside Police Department
Orange Police Department
Richmond Police Department
Riverside County Sheriff's Office
Salina Police Department
San Diego County Sheriff's Office
San Diego Police Department
San Francisco Police Department
San Jose Police Department
San Mateo County Sheriff's Office
Sonoma County Sheriff's Office
Southern Alameda County Gang Task Force

COLORADO

Aurora Police Department
Colorado Springs Police Department
Denver Police Department
Fort Collins Police Department
Grand Junction Police Department
Greeley Police Department
Mesa County Sheriff's Office
Pueblo Police Department

Connecticut

Connecticut Department of Corrections
Meriden Police Department
New Haven Police Department
Putnam Police Departments
Stamford Police Department
Windsor Police Department

Delaware

Delaware State Police

District of Columbia

Metropolitan Police Department

Florida

Alachua County Sheriff's Office
Brevard County Sheriff's Office
Broward County Sheriff's Office
Florida Department of Corrections
Florida Department of Law Enforcement
Florida Office of the Attorney General
Florida Gang Reduction Strategy
Gadsden County Sheriff's Office
Gainesville Police Department
Hernando County Sheriff's Office
Hillsborough County Sheriff's Office
Lake County Sheriff's Office
Lakeland Police Department
Miami-Dade Police Department
Orange County Sheriff's Office
Orlando Police Department
Pasco County Sheriff's Office
Polk County Sheriff's Office
Sarasota Police Department
Seminole County Sheriff's Office
St. Lucie County Sheriff's Office
Volusia County Sheriff's Office

Georgia

Albany Police Department
Athens Police Department

Atlanta Police Department
Columbia Police Department
Macon Police Department
Marietta Police Department

Hawaii

Hawaii County Police Department
Hawaii Department of Corrections

Idaho

Ada County Sheriff's Office
American Falls Police Department
Bannock County Sheriff's Department
Bonneville County Juvenile Detention
Bonneville County Sheriff's Department
Caldwell Police Department
Canyon County Sheriff's Office
Cassia County Sheriff's Department
Idaho Board of Correction, Evaluation and Compliance
Idaho Criminal Justice Commission
Idaho Department of Corrections
Idaho Falls Police Department
Jerome Police Department
Nampa Police Department
Rupert Police Department
Twin Falls Sheriff's Department

Illinois

Cook County Sheriff's Office

Iowa

Cedar Rapids Police Department
Des Moines Police Department
Sioux City Police Department

Kansas

Dodge City Police Department
Garden City Police Department
Grand Island Police Department
Kansas City Police Department
Salinas Police Department

Topeka Police Department
Wichita Police Department

Kentucky

Bowling Green Police Department
Frankfort Police Department
Lexington Police Department
Owensboro Police Department

Louisiana

Louisiana State Police
Shreveport Police Department

Maine

Lewiston Police Department
Portland Police Department

Maryland

Baltimore Police Department
Frederick Police Department
Hampstead Police Department
Salisbury Police Department

Massachusetts

Chelmsford Police Department
Fall River Police Department
Framingham Police Department
Lowell Police Department
Lynn Police Department New
Bedford Police Department
Springfield Police Department
Worcester Police Department

Michigan

Detroit Police Department
Flint Police Department
Kent County Sheriff's Office
Saginaw Police Department

Minnesota
- Metro Gang Strike Task Force

Missouri
- Columbia Police Department
- Independence Police Department
- Joplin Police Department
- Kansas City Police Department
- Springfield Police Department
- St. Louis County Police Department
- St. Louis Police Department

Montana
- Billings Police Department
- Cascade County Department of Corrections
- Cascade County Sheriff's Department
- Great Falls Police Department
- Missoula Police Department
- Montana All Threat Intelligence Center
- Montana Department of Corrections
  - Pine Hills Youth Correctional Facility
- Yellowstone County Sheriff's Department

Nebraska
- Bellevue Police Department
- Grand Island Police Department
- Lincoln Police Department
- Omaha Police Department

Nevada
- Las Vegas Police Department
- Reno Police Department

New Hampshire
- Manchester Police Department
- Nashua Police Department
- Rochester Police Department

New Jersey
- Essex County Gang Unit

Jersey City Police Department
Mercer County Prosecutors Office
Newark Police Department
Passaic County Prosecutor's Office
Trenton Police Department
Union County Prosecutor
Intelligence Unit

New Mexico

Albuquerque Police Department
Carlsbad Police Department
Las Cruces Police Department
Santa Fe Police Department

New York

Albany Police Department
Binghamton Police Department
Buffalo Police Department
New York City Police Department
New York State Police
Rochester Police Department
Syracuse Police Department
White Plains Police Department

North Carolina

Durham Police Department
Fayetteville Police Department
Greensboro Police Department
North Carolina Department of Crime Control and Public Safety
Raleigh Police Department
Winston-Salem Police Department

North Dakota

Bismarck Police Department
Fargo Police Department

Ohio

Akron Police Department
Cleveland Police Department
Columbus Police Department
Dayton Police Department

Youngstown Police Department

Oklahoma

Lawton Police Department
Oklahoma City Police Department
Tulsa Police Department

Oregon

Clackamas County Sheriff's Office
Eugene Police Department
Fairview Police Department
Gresham Police Department
Medford Police Department
Multnomah County Sheriff's Office
Oregon Department of Justice
Portland Police Department
Salem Police Department
Troutdale Police Department
Washington County Sheriff's Office

Pennsylvania

Allentown Police Department
Erie Police Department
Hermitage Police Department
Lancaster Police Department
Philadelphia Police Department
Pittsburgh Police Department
Reading Police Department
Scranton Police Department

Rhode Island

Providence Police Department
Rhode Island State Police
West Warwick Police Department

South Carolina

Charleston Police Department
Columbia Police Department
Greenville Police Department
North Charleston Police Department
South Carolina Department of Corrections

South Carolina Gang Prevention Study Committee
Spartanburg Police Department
York County Sheriff's Office

South Dakota

Rapid City Police Department
Sioux Falls Police Department

Tennessee

Chattanooga Police Department
Murfreesboro Police Department
Nashville Police Department

Texas

Brownsville Police Department
Corpus Christi Police Department
Dallas Police Department
Department of Public Safety
Eagle Pass Police Department
Ector County Sheriff's Office
El Paso Police Department
Houston Police Department
Joint Operational Intelligence Center
Laredo Police Department
McAllen Police Department
Midland Police Department
Odessa Police Department
San Antonio Police Department

Utah

Cedar City Police Department
Garfield County Drug Task Force
Iron County Drug Task Force
Ogden Police Department/ Weber County Gang Unit
Salt Lake City Police Department
Salt Lake County Area Gang Project
St. George Police Department
Washington County Drug Task Force

Virginia

Fairfax Police Department

Fredericksburg Police Department
Henrico County Police Department
Loudon City Police Department
Richmond Police Department
Virginia State Police

Washington

Clark County Gang Task Force
King County Sheriff's Office
Pierce County Sheriff's Office
Seattle Police Department
Skamania County Gang Task Force
Snohomish County Sheriff's Office
Spokane Police Department
Tacoma Police Department
Washington Department of Corrections

West Virginia

Charleston Police Department
Morgantown Police Department
Wheeling Police Department

Wisconsin

Brown County Drug Task Force
Cudahy Police Department
Dane County Sheriff's Office
Dodge County Sheriff's Office
Eau Claire Police Department
Greendale Police Department
Hales Corner Police Department
Janesville Police Department
Jefferson County Drug Task Force
Kenosha Police Department
Madison Police Department
Milwaukee Police Department
Rock County Sheriff's Office
Sheboygan Police Department

Wyoming

Casper Police Department
Cheyenne Police Department

Rawlins Police Department

OTHER

Canada Border Services Agency
Criminal Intelligence Services Canada
International Outlaw Motorcycle Gang Investigators Association
National Alliance of Gang Investigators' Associations
National Center for Educational Statistics

Made in United States
Troutdale, OR
11/03/2026

56844461R00035